Kahuta: The Indo-Israeli Plan to Attack Pakistan's Nuclear Plant

SAGHIR IQBAL

ISBN: 9781791811037

DEDICATION

I dedicate this book to all those who gave me encouragement, support and guidance. Foremost, to my parents, from whom I have learnt so much.

CONTENTS

1 Security Issues... Pg 8

2 The plan to destroy Kahuta nuclear plant.............. Pg 29

3 Interception of the plan .... Pg 35

4 Indo-Israeli pre-emptive strike......................... Pg 42

5 References... Pg 50

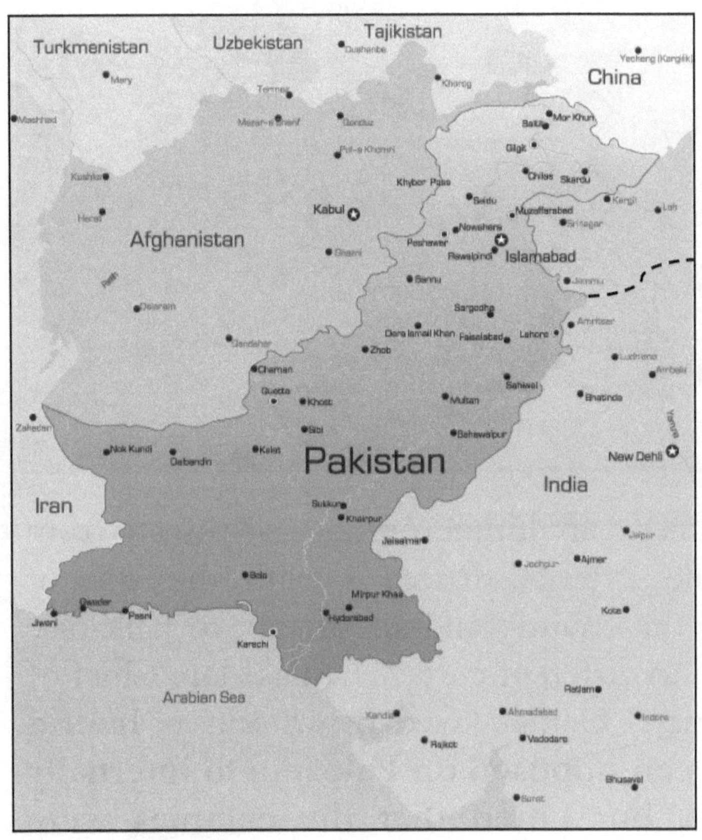

Pakistan Map[1]

---

[1] http://www.beautifulholidays.com.au/travel-guide/asia/pakistan/index.php

Pakistan faces a multitude number of threats from internal and external forces – with the aim of weakening the country and an attempt to balkanise Pakistan in to different parts. The Pakistani Chief of Army, General Qamar Javed Bajwa said a **"hybrid war had been imposed on Pakistan to internally weaken it, but noted that the enemies were failing to divide the country on the basis of ethnicity and other identities"**.

Furthermore he states, **"Our enemies know that they cannot beat us fair and square and have thus subjected us to a cruel, evil and protracted hybrid war. They are trying to weaken our resolve by weakening us from within"**.[2]

According to the writer and analyst Dr Farrukh Saleem, a Hybrid war has been imposed on Pakistan. He states that Pakistan is under an eight dimensional attack that has been waged under various strategies as follows:

(1) Economic warfare;
(2) Foreign support of domestic unrest
(3) Information warfare propaganda
(4) Diplomatic onslaught
(5) Cyber attacks
(6) Offensive from irregular forces
(7) Operations by Special Forces
(8) Regular military operations.[3]

There are 3 dimensions that this attack is based on:

(1) Economic
(2) Political
(3) Societal.

The aim of Pakistan's adversaries are to weaken the nation's economy so that it is unable to allocate

---

[2] 'Hybrid war' imposed on country to internally weaken it, says Bajwa (15 April 2018), https://www.dawn.com/news/1401747

[3] Pakistan under hybrid war attack from eight dimensions (2018) https://timesofislamabad.com/22-Apr-2018/pakistan-under-hybrid-war-attack-from-eight-dimensions

adequate resources for its defence needs. A constant pressure is exerted so that the country continues to borrow money and get into the debt-trap. Hence International trade and debt is utilised as a weapon of war.

Furthermore, weak and corrupt governments are supported so that weak and ineffective governments are used to keep the progress of the country down. It is argued that weak governments are more prone to incorporate unsound economic projects that will further cause economic instability in the country. In addition, weaknesses in Pakistan's society are being exploited to cause further unrest/divisions and possible desire of splitting the country (as was in the case of Pakistan being dismembered by India's support for disgruntled groups in the past when it lost the former East Pakistan to Bangladesh).

There are widespread evidence that the attempt to further dismember Pakistan has been implanted by a number of countries such as the USA and India (with the support and help of their respective allies).[4]

The writer and analyst Andrew Korybko further states that the Hybrid War on Pakistan has been intensified by countries such as the USA to damage

---

[4] Ibid.

its International relations and standing. He gives the following opinion, **"it can be expected that the US and its global Mainstream Media partners will reframe everything in the reverse by making the world think that the Pakistani victims are really the aggressors and that the Americans are completely innocent of any wrongdoing".** [5]

It is argued that Pakistan's adversaries are successfully operating the various hybrid warfare methods to 'bleed' the country. Due to the inability of these foreign powers to coerce Pakistan with their conventional and nuclear arsenals – they have chosen the hybrid warfare route. Pakistan's enemies are making alliances and devising new trade routes in order to isolate Pakistan and robustly continue to propagate sophisticated propaganda against it and also finance militants to cause widespread instability and terrorist activities to further damage the country's stability.[6]

---

[5] Andrew Korybko (2018), Pakistan And America Are In The Throes Of A Serious Diplomatic Crisis:
https://orientalreview.org/2018/05/19/pakistan-and-america-are-in-the-throes-of-a-serious-diplomatic-crisis/

[6] Dr Zafar Nawaz Jaspal (Associate Professor, School of Politics and International Relations), Hybrid warfare's menace (2017) https://pakobserver.net/hybrid-warfares-menace

Pakistani Main Battle Tank

Pakistan's main threat perceptions emanate from India. Its main concerns include India's military build-up, both conventionally and nuclear, and its ability to deliver nuclear payloads due to its ever-increasing ballistic capabilities (including the Prithvi and Agni surface-to-surface missiles and nuclear capable IAF fighters). India now has the nuclear command-and-control centres required to integrate nuclear weapons and related assets. Its Akash anti-missile missile, claimed to be superior to the US Patriot, is also being positioned to intercept incoming Ghauri and Hatf missiles, which has created another security headache for Pakistan's defence planners.[7]

India's assertive posture since the 1971 war has

[7] News International, Armed to the Teeth, Jang Publishers Ltd, 1998, Pg10

increased in the last few years, particularly following the advent of the BJP fundamentalist government. Although the BJP government has attempted to explain that India's military build-up is defensive and commensurate with India's overall economic growth, others in the region cannot be so sure of India's intentions.[8]

Pakistan is also concerned about potential threats emanating from other regions, such as Israel. The reported joint Indo-Israeli pre-emptive strike intended to destroy its nuclear facilities and the frequent reports of air incursion by Israeli and Indian aircraft, have only served to highlight Pakistani fears. There is also much more concern over the exporting of sophisticated Israeli military hardware and the close collaboration in nuclear ties between these two countries.[9] America's decision to impose punitive sanctions against Pakistan over its nuclear programme has also aggrieved the Pakistan government, which argues that it had no feasible option but to test, given the insufficient promises of aid from some western governments, after India revived its nuclear programme. Pakistan was unwilling to ditch its nuclear programme, after <u>weighing up the options</u>, as the inducement to not

[8] Johann Mcgeary, India's Surprise Nuclear Tests, The Time, May 25, 1998, Pg34

[9] Christopher Walker, Israel Helped India for 20 Years, The Times, Thursday June 4, 1998, Pg16

test was not sufficient to safeguard its security. In the past, the cruise missile attacks against Osama Bin Laden in Afghanistan also crossed Pakistan air space, further deteriorating the relationship with America.[10]

The US war on terror has further destabilised the region and Pakistan is feeling the 'heat' from a so called ally that is seen to be ditching Pakistan and wooing India – allegedly to contain a rising China. The deliberate attack on Pakistani border post in which a number of Pakistani soldiers were killed, showed how quickly things can change.

However, tensions exist primarily with India and Pakistan and the future looks bleak, with numerous occasions where war has been imminent, usually over Kashmir. With the advanced military equipment incorporated into their respective armies and the acquisition of weapons of mass destruction (especially their nuclear capability), there is a serious risk of a nuclear war occurring between these two neighbours in the very near future.

---

[10] Umer Farooq, Striking Consequences, Janes Defence Weekly, 2 September 1998, Pg23

Pakistan's Shaheen 3 Nuclear capable ballistic missile

The 1981 Israeli Strike - Operation Opera

On the 7th of June, 1981, the world's first successful air strike on a nuclear plant was conducted. Prime Minister Menachem Begin of Israel had given the orders to destroy the nuclear plant near Baghdad.[11] Operation Opera (also known as Operation Babylon) had resulted in Israel launching a pre-emptive strike on the French built Osirak Nuclear reactor at the Tuwaitha complex in Iraq. Israel

---

[11]   1981: Israel bombs Baghdad nuclear reactor - http://news.bbc.co.uk/onthisday/hi/dates/stories/june/7/newsid_3014000/3014 623.stm

believed that this nuclear plant was designed to make nuclear weapons that would eventually be used to destroy Israel.

Israel and Iraq Map[12]

The air strike was undertaken by eight Israeli F-16 Falcon combat aircraft, which dropped 16 2,000 pound bombs on the nuclear reactor. The F-16s

pl/hi/middle_east/02/iraq_events/html/israeli

were escorted by six F-15 Eagle aircraft for protection from any enemy fighter aircraft. The aircraft flew low and had evaded detection by Saudi air defences and also the US Airborne Early-Warning and Control Systems (AWACS) aircraft that were temporarily based in Saudi Arabia.[13]

The aircraft had flown 600 miles over Jordanian, Saudi and Iraqi airspace to attack the reactor.[14] Ten Iraqi soldiers and one French Engineer were killed in the attack. The Israeli's suffered no losses, despite encountering enemy firepower on its return journey.[15]

---

[13] A Lesson from the 1981 Raid on Osirak - https://www.wilsoncenter.org/blog-post/lesson-the-1981-raid-osirak

[14] An Israeli attack against Iran would backfire — just like Israel's 1981 strike on Iraq - https://www.washingtonpost.com/opinions/an-israeli-attack-against-iran-would-backfire--just-like-israels-1981-strike-on-iraq/2012/02/28/gIQATOMFnR_story.html?utm_term=.926ab686893f

[15] In 1981, Israel's Deadly Air Force Took out Saddam Hussein's Only Nuclear Reactor - https://nationalinterest.org/blog/the-buzz/1981-israels-deadly-air-force-took-out-saddam-husseins-only-25058

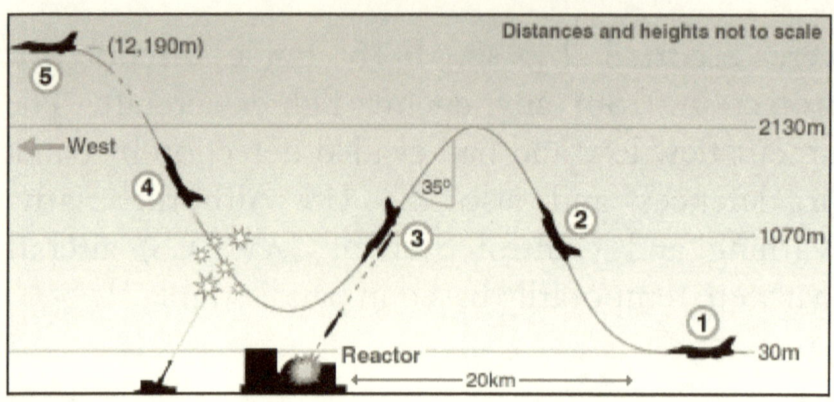

Bombing mission[16]

The Israeli's had found out the blind spots from the Jordanian, Saudi and Iraqi airspaces. The Israeli combat aircraft had dropped their heavily laden fuel tanks on the route in Saudi Arabian airspace. The Iraqis had not anticipated any threat from this particular corridor, they were more focused on their war with Iran (during the 1980 Iran-Iraq war).

In addition, it is alleged that the Iranians had given the Israeli's photographic evidence on the plant. Iran had conducted its own operation against the plant but was not able to destroy it (Operation Scorch Sword had only damaged it). It did take reconnaissance missions by its F-4E Phantom fighter jets.

---

[16] Factfile: How Osirak was bombed -
http://news.bbc.co.uk/1/hi/world/middle_east/5020778.stm

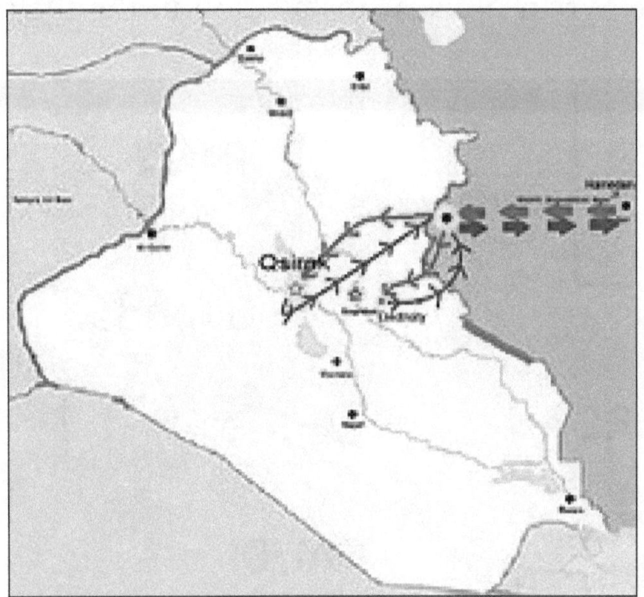

Iran's Operation Scorch Sword[17]

The Israeli plan was meticulously conducted and
well planned – a difficult mission was successfully
completed. It was a triumph for Israel and big
setback for Iraq. In two minutes, the dome of the
Osirak nuclear plant has been completely destroyed.[18]
It also demonstrated Israeli tenacity, skill and
success in these type of operations.

This episode was further repeated 26 years later in
Syria. On September 6, 2007 Israel had conducted
'Operation Orchard' where it had successfully

---

[17] https://en.wikipedia.org/wiki/Operation_Scorch_Sword

[18] 36 Years Ago today, "Operation Opera": The Israeli Air Strike on an Iraqi
Nuclear Reactor - https://theaviationist.com/2017/06/07/36-years-ago-today-
operation-opera-the-israeli-air-strike-on-an-iraqi-nuclear-reactor/

destroyed the Syrian Nuclear installation in the Deir ez-Zor area.[19]

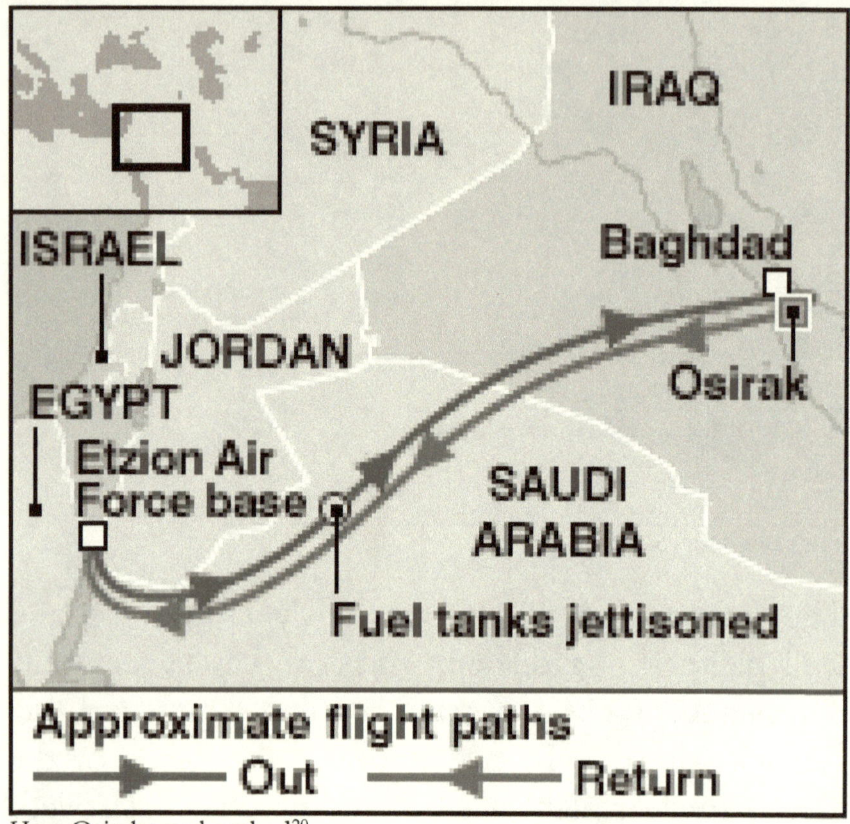

How Osirak was bombed[20]

Operation 'Kahuta'

---

[19] 36 Years Ago today, "Operation Opera": The Israeli Air Strike on an Iraqi Nuclear Reactor - https://theaviationist.com/2017/06/07/36-years-ago-today-operation-opera-the-israeli-air-strike-on-an-iraqi-nuclear-reactor/

[20] Factfile: How Osirak was bombed - http://news.bbc.co.uk/1/hi/world/middle_east/5020778.stm

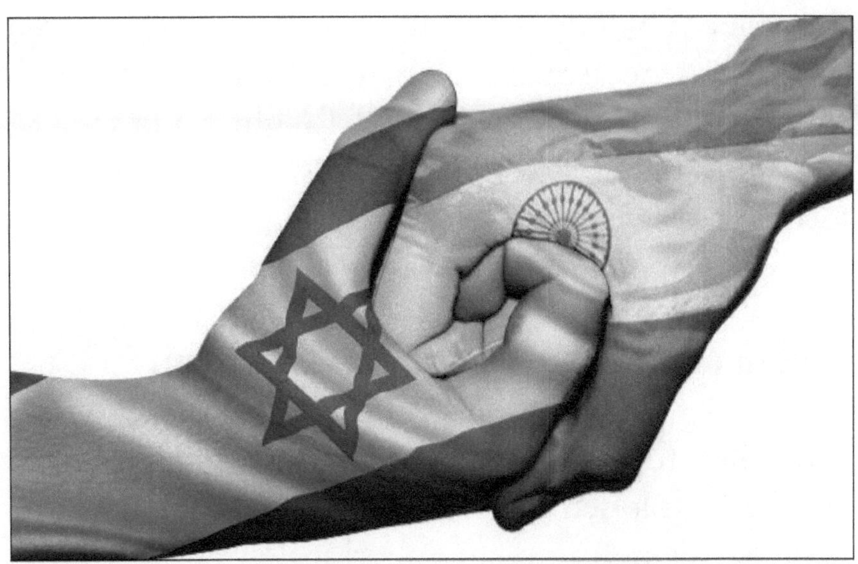

There are strong evidences that a joint Indo-Israeli attack on Pakistan's nuclear facilities had been planned since the early 1980s. Israel was concerned on the close ties that Pakistan had enjoyed with the Arab countries in the region. The Israeli plan to destroy the Pakistani nuclear reactor carried more risks due to the distance and geography of the Pakistani nuclear plant. The Israeli aircraft would be required to fly over 1000 miles, mainly over a number of Arab countries. It would require a lot more combat aircraft and air-to-air refuelling tankers.

They would then have to circumvent Pakistani air defences and then drop the bombs on the Kahuta Nuclear reactor. This task would stretch the Israeli capability and the attack may be less effective than the strike it had done on the Osirak plant. This then prompted the Israeli's to plan a joint attack with India (India and Pakistan had fought a number of wars and had issues in regards to the disputed territory of Kashmir).

Indian attempts to destroy Kahuta plant

India has fought a number of wars with Pakistan and had exploded its own nuclear bomb in 1974. It had also helped in dismembering Pakistan in 1971, in which East Pakistan became Bangladesh. The dismemberment of Pakistan had given it the resolve to pursue the nuclear path - as a deterrence against a numerical superior adversary.

India had enjoyed conventional superiority in regards to combat aircrafts, tanks, naval ships and manpower. It now enjoyed a nuclear capability – in fear of this, Pakistan had embarked on a mission to develop a nuclear device to address the power of balance in South Asia.

India had feared that a Pakistani nuclear device would neutralise its conventional superiority and had therefore contemplated of attacking Pakistan's nuclear facility at Kahuta.

Declassified top-secret documents from 1984-85 via the US State Department indicated that an attack had nearly taken place. The US had warned Pakistan about an Indian attack on its nuclear reactor. The US was worried that any attack would divert attention from the Afghanistan conflict in which Pakistan was playing a major part in helping the resistance movement against the then Soviet Union forces.[21]

In addition, rumours began to circulate across different parts of the world. It was alleged that the Soviet Union was discussing this with the Hungarians. The US daily the 'Washington Post' had run a front-page story on December 20, 1982 headlined, **'India said to eye raid on Pakistan's A-plants'**.[22]

With the inception of the Anglo-French Jaguar attack fighter aircraft in service, the Indian Air Force (IAF) had conducted a study on the feasibility of attacking the Kahuta nuclear plant in June 1981. The study indicated that the Kahuta plant could be

---

[21] India, Israel almost attacked Kahuta: report -
https://www.pakistantoday.com.pk/2015/10/26/india-israel-almost-attacked-kahuta-report/

[22] India Said to Eye Raid on Pakistani A-Plants -
https://www.washingtonpost.com/archive/politics/1982/12/20/india-said-to-eye-raid-on-pakistani-a-plants/7e30dde5-e97c-45dc-82bb-521dee37a6ac/?noredirect=on&utm_term=.bdaddcfe8110

successfully destroyed but it would initiate a full scale war between India and Pakistan.

Furthermore there were fears that the Pakistan Air Force (PAF) would respond in kind and attack Indian nuclear reactors, such as the one in Trombay. Accordingly, the Pakistani nuclear scientist Munir Ahmed Khan had met Indian Atomic Energy Commission chief-designate Raja Ramanna at an international meet in Vienna and conveyed a message that a retaliatory strike on Bhabha Atomic Research Centre at Trombay would be taking place for sure if Kahuta was attacked.[23]

It was alleged that Indian intelligence agencies (RAW) and the Israeli Mossad were cooperating on helping each other in regards to building a picture of the Kahuta plan. In February 1983 Indian military officials had bought electronic warfare equipment to neutralise Kahuta's air defences. India had also received the technical details of the PAFs US F-16 Falcon combat aircraft (the most sophisticated aircraft in Pakistan's arsenal at the time) in exchange for details on the Soviet MIG-23 Flogger combat aircraft (that was becoming in service in countries such as Syria).

---

[23] India, Israel almost attacked Kahuta: report -
https://www.pakistantoday.com.pk/2015/10/26/india-israel-almost-attacked-kahuta-report/

Indian military advisors proposal for an attack in March 1982 was not carried out by the then Indian Prime Minister Indira Gandhi due to a number of reasons.

Moreover in September 1984, India again had considered striking the Kahuta plant. Declassified documents stated that the US Ambassador Dean Hinton told President Zia of Pakistan that there were signs of India preparing for an attack on Kahuta. This resulted in the element of surprise being lost as Pakistan bolstered its defence sites around Kahuta.

Rumours of a joint attack by both nations were becoming widespread. The joint attack would destroy the so-called 'Islamic bomb' being developed by Pakistan. The Israeli Air force was to lead the joint attack.

Accordingly, the Israeli aircraft were to be staged from Jamnagar airfield in Gujarat, refuel at a satellite airfield in North India and track the Himalayas to avoid early radar detection, but the Indian Prime Minister Indira Gandhi eventually vetoed the idea.[24]

---

[24] India, Israel almost attacked Kahuta: report -
https://www.pakistantoday.com.pk/2015/10/26/india-israel-almost-attacked-kahuta-report/

Denial by both nations

Both India and Israel had denied that they had ever planned an attack on Pakistan's nuclear facilities. However, the evidence suggests that a concrete plan had been agreed on a number of occasions but did not go through due to a number of sound reasons.[25]

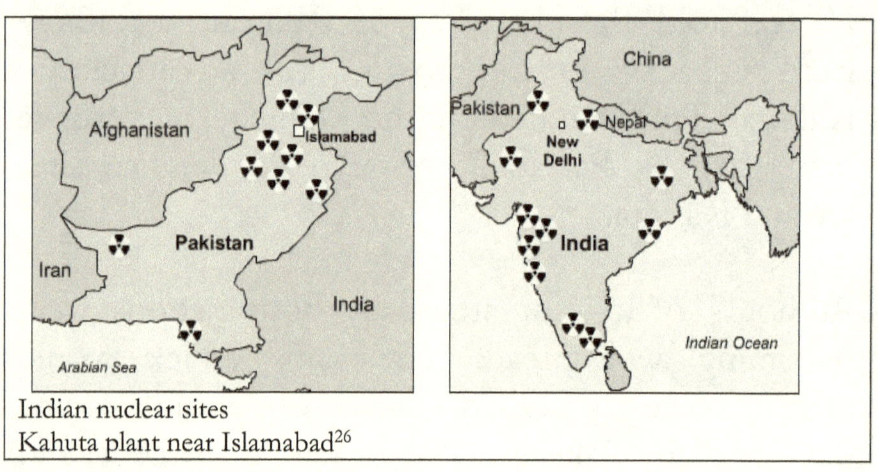

Indian nuclear sites
Kahuta plant near Islamabad[26]

---

[25] Israelis dismiss claims of plans to blow up Pakistani nuclear sites - https://www.irishtimes.com/news/israelis-dismiss-claims-of-plans-to-blow-up-pakistani-nuclear-sites-1.159410

[26] http://www.atomicarchive.com/Reports/India/PakistanFacilities_static.shtml

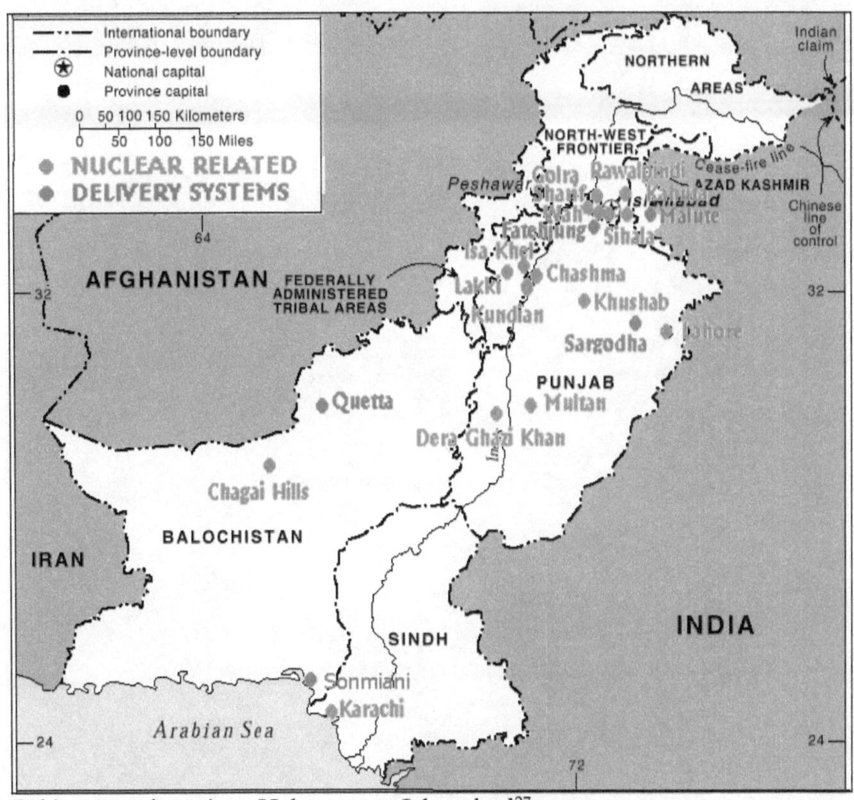

Pakistan nuclear sites, Kahuta near Islamabad[27]

---

[27] http://poster.4teachers.org/view/poster.php?poster_id=337240

Indian Air Force major air bases[28]

---

[28] https://www.indiatoday.in/india/north/story/indian-air-force-begins-its-largest-ever-wargames-156329-2013-03-17

2 THE PLAN TO DESTROY KAHUTA NUCLEAR PLANT

Indian Prime minister Modi and Israeli Prime minister Netanyahu.

Pakistan has faced numerous challenges and threats to its security. It has faced orchestrated state terrorism on its soil and has had a number of nations trying their best to destabilise the country. There have been consistent attempts to destroy any economic and military strength of this nation through a number of schemes and plots.

An external threat to its security has come from a number of countries. For instance, Pakistan's security concern is the improving military ties between India and Israel. Since formal ties were established in 1992, Israeli military exports to India have grown to over $150 million a year. From the period 2012-2016 Israeli firms sold up to $1 billion a year in sales to India on average. In fiscal 2016-18, Israel is trying to sell the sophisticated Spike anti-tank missiles - if India goes through with this deal, Israel will be for the first time the largest arms supplier to India.[29] The defence co-operation includes sophisticated pilot-less drones, night vision equipment and extending to the nuclear, ballistic missile targeting systems and spy satellite technology.[30]

India-Israel ties increased military ties and the sales of sophisticated items to the Indian armed forces has caused a lot of concern to Pakistan. Force multiplier Israeli technologies have been sold to India and agreements in development projects of military related equipment has also increased. Pakistan is especially worried about the sale of the state-of-the-art Arrow anti-missile system that gives India the potential to neutralize part of Pakistan's nuclear ballistic missile capability. In addition, the Phalcon Airborne Early Warning, Command and Control (AEW&C) system will give India the deep edge and capability to look deep into Pakistan's

---

[29] Israel likely to become India's largest arms supplier - https://www.hindustantimes.com/world-news/israel-likely-to-become-india-s-largest-arms-supplier/story-tZQFenVzYWzaQFnPqbznqM.html

[30] Yoel Cohen, India bomb test may affect Israel Relations, Jewish Chronicle, Publishers Jewish Chronical Newspaper Ltd, May 29, 1998, Pg3

territory (it gives India the ability to easily detect the movement of Pakistan's combat aircraft). Also the co-development of the Barak Anti-missile system will gives the Indian Navy huge advantage in its defensive and offensive capability.[31]

Israeli made Phalcon AWACS on a IL-76 Aircraft of the Indian Air Force

Israel has viewed that Pakistani nuclear programme with a growing sense of alarm since the 1970s. It fears an 'Islamic Bomb' either being deployed to counter Israel's nuclear and conventional security over its Arab foes, or being transferred to an Arab country.[32] In 1981, Prime Minister Sharon of Israel indicated that the security of the Israeli entity included Pakistan.[33]

---

[31] India-Israel Strengthened Nexus -
http://hilal.gov.pk/index.php/layouts/item/2805-india-israel-strengthened-nexus
[32] Ibid

Kahuta nuclear plant in Pakistan

There has been constant double standards and discrimination when it came to Pakistan developing a nuclear device. Pakistan's bomb was given a religious dimension by most western nations (a deliberate scaremongering campaign). Pakistan's bomb was called an 'Islamic Bomb', however this religious context was never given to the Israeli bomb as a 'Jewish Bomb' or India's bomb as an 'Hindu Bomb' or even the USA's bomb as a 'Christian Bomb' or the Soviet Union's bomb as a ' Communist Bomb or Atheist bomb'.[34] This deliberate attempt was to malign Pakistan and justify an attack on this country.

---

[33] Y. Ammar, The Kashmir Factor, Palestine Times, 9 October, 1991, Pg2

[34] How safe are Pakistan`s nuclear assets- https://www.dawn.com/news/1310835

According to the journalists Adrian Levy and Catherine Scott-Clark (in their book titled '*Deception: Pakistan, the US and the Global Weapons Conspiracy*' claimed that in 1983-84 India and Israel secretly planned to attack Pakistan's nuclear facility in Kahuta (near Islamabad).[35]

Israel had attempted to destroy the Kahuta plant as it had successfully destroyed the Iraqi nuclear plant in Osirak. It needed Indian help in undertaking this mission. There were strong ties between the Israeli Mossad and Indian RAW intelligence agencies. Both countries had felt that it was in their interest to undergo a preventive strike on Pakistani nuclear facility in Kahuta. A number of plans were initiated in 1982 to 1984 by Israel and India in regards to implementing this attack – however due to a number of reasons it did not take place.

---

[35] India, Israel almost attacked Kahuta: report -
https://www.pakistantoday.com.pk/2015/10/26/india-israel-almost-attacked-kahuta-report/

Israeli US made F-16 combat aircraft attacking Iraqi Osiraq nuclear plant

F-16 combat aircraft

3 INTERCEPTION OF THE PLAN

Pakistani intelligence (ISI) had intercepted the communication of the Indo-Israeli joint plan of attacking Pakistan's Kahuta facility and took appropriate security measures. Pakistan had sent strong messages to Tel Aviv and New Delhi that if Kahuta is attacked by anyone they would lay nuclear waste on Tel Aviv and New Delhi.

Pakistani ISI Emblem

Pakistan's defences were put on a full alert and the Pakistani air force was put on high alert for any incursions. It is said that the PAF Chief of Air Staff had asked the Pakistani F-16 squadron if any pilot was willing to volunteer to fly a one way mission to Tel Aviv (Pakistan couldn't have flown a sortie to Israel as it lacked air-to-air-refuelling at the time), the whole PAF F-16 squadron raised their hands to volunteer.

Air Marshal M. Anwar Shamim (PAF Air Chief during that time), narrated "that while talk of the India-Israel nexus was still in the air, he requested Foreign Minister Sahibzada Yaqub Ali Khan to declare at an appropriate time Pakistan's intention of retaliating if any action was taken against the country's nuclear assets".

IAF Jaguars in conjunction with Israeli F-16s were to be the key aircraft to attack Pakistan's nuclear facility in Kahuta.

In addition, in 1983 Dr Raja Ramanna, the then director of the Bhabha Atomic Research Centre,

was warned by the then Chairman of Pakistan
Atomic Energy Commission Munir Ahmed Khan in
Vienna in the autumn of 1983 that Islamabad would
attack Trombay (Indian nuclear plant) if its facilities
in Kahuta were hit.

IAF Jaguar attack aircraft

Furthermore, it is claimed that US intelligence
satellites had detected two Jaguar squadrons missing
from Indian Ambala airbase in Indian Punjab and
moved to another location close to the Kahuta
facility near Islamabad. The information was also
proved to Pakistan, reducing the element of surprise
from a joint Indo-Israeli attack.

The joint Indo-Israeli collusion was said to be

planned since the early 1980s. It was alleged that a full-scale mock-up of Kahuta facility was built in the Negev desert by Israel. This was done via the use satellite pictures and intelligence. Israeli pilots in their F-16/F-15 combat aircraft had practised mock attacks.[36]

Other reports that were coming out, stated that Israel also contemplated an air strike directly from mainland Israel. Israel was planning to refuel its aircraft via refuelling tanker aircrafts and once it had reached midway it planned to shoot down a commercial airline's flight over the Indian Ocean.

The commercial air liner would be travelling to Islamabad airport. The Israeli warplanes will be flying in a tight formation so that they appeared as one large aircraft on Pakistan's radar screens. They would use the downed commercial airliners call sign to enter Pakistan airspace, this would prevent detection. The warplanes would then strike the Kahuta plant (near Islamabad) and then fly over to Indian occupied Kashmir in Jammu to refuel and then exit.

However, this mission was aborted once Israel realised that the Pakistani ground defences and air defence fighters were on constant combat air

---

[36] How safe are Pakistan`s nuclear assets- https://www.dawn.com/news/1310835

patrols throughout Pakistan.

It was stated that Pakistan had conveyed the message that it would lay waste to Israel's Dimona nuclear reactor in the Negev desert. It would also attack India's Trombay nuclear reactor. Finally, India's Prime minister Indira Gandhi had stopped the operation, which had disappointed the military planners in New Delhi and Jerusalem."[37]

Israels nuclear sites[38]

[37] How safe are Pakistan`s nuclear assets- https://www.dawn.com/news/1310835

[38] https://fanack.com/nuclear-programs/israel/

Israeli dimona nuclear plant[39]

To Pakistani officials, the signs were clear – their nuclear facilities were under the threat of a preventive strike. Both the Karachi Nuclear Power Plant (KANUPP) and Kahuta were vulnerable, so President Zia tasked Chief of General Staff Mirza Aslam Beg to improve their defences. PAF planes scrambled and began combat air patrol (CAP missions), which soon became a part of the normal operational routine. Since then, the skies above Kahuta have been no- fly zones

---

[39] https://www.theguardian.com/world/2014/jan/15/truth-israels-secret-nuclear-arsenal

PAF Mirage combat aircraft

PAF US made F-16 Fighting Falcon combat aircraft

4 INDO-ISRAELI PRE-EMPTIVE STRIKE

In the 1980s, there were reports in both the British and Indian media of Israel requesting Indian co-operation to bomb the Kahuta reactor in Pakistan. This would have involved the use of the Indian air base at Jamnagar near the Pakistan border as a possible refuelling stop. India reportedly declined the request due to the fear of a Pakistani retaliation on its own nuclear sites.[40]

Moreover in 1991, Pakistan's Interior Ministry warned Parliament of another possible joint Israeli-Indian sabotage attempt at Kahuta, which is only 20km from the Srinagar capital of Indian-held Kashmir.[41]

---

[40] Cohen, op cit:3
[41] Ammar, op cit:4

Israeli US F-16 combat aircraft

According to the Indian weekly *'News Behind News'*, Major General Ivry, the second-in-command of the Israeli Defence Ministry, attempted another Israeli-Indian collaboration in 1995. He requested the use of Indian airbases at Jodhpur or Bhuj, on the basis of a *'common threat perception'*, in return for an Israeli package deal to India which included airborne warning and control systems (AWACS), remotely piloted vehicles (RPV), sophisticated radar jammers and specialised weapons, including parts of its own spy satellite technology. India turned down this package, which would almost certainly have raised fears of a Pakistani retaliation on India's own reactors.[42]

[42] News International, Israel offers India AWACS for Airbases as Part of 'Common Threat Perception', Jang Publishers Ltd, April 18, 1995, Pg1

Of greater concern was Israeli-Indian nuclear co-operation. Dr Abdul Kalam, the architect of India's nuclear and ballistic missile programme, visited Israel several times, over a period of months between 1996-1997. Senior Israeli scientists also made several visits to India over the same period. The close ties between Dr Kalam and his Israeli counterparts have suggested parallels with Israel's secret co-operation with South Africa in at least one nuclear test in the late 1970s.[43]

Israeli F-15 Eagle combat aircraft

---

[43] Christopher Walker, Israel's Helped India for 20 Years, The Times, Thursday June 4, 1998, Pg16

Israeli US supplied F-16 multi-role combat aircraft

According to *The Washington Times,* Pakistan feared a combined Indo-Israeli pre-emptive air-strike as it conducted its first nuclear test on 28th May 1998, in the same way that Israeli combat aircraft destroyed Iraq's Osirak nuclear reactor in 1981.[44] An F-16 fighter-bomber was spotted twice in Pakistan's airspace just before the tests. The aircraft was assumed to be part of an Israeli strike-force, as India has no F-16 aircraft in its air force. Pakistan, suspecting that Israeli jets were using Indian bases, made preparations to counter an air-strike by placing its air-force and missiles on high alert.[45]

---

[44] Martin Sieff and Yoel Cohen, Pakistan Feared Israel's Strike during Nuclear test, Jewish Chronical, June 5, 1998, Pg3

Western defence experts did not rule out the possibility of an Indo-Israeli attack on Pakistan's nuclear facilities. According to Paul Beaver, of Jane's Information Group, the Israeli F-16s had been equipped with an advanced reconnaissance system to take high-altitude pictures of targets over a 50 miles radius. The high resolution pictures were capable of reading the lettering on the side of a truck parked at Pakistani nuclear facility.[46]

Israeli F-16 multi-role combat aircraft

Overall, Israel's offers of advance weapon systems, her help with India's nuclear and ballistic missile programme and also her assistance in providing

---

[45] Christopher Walker and Michael Evans, Pakistan Feared Israeli Raid, The Times, Wednesday June 3, 1998, Pg3

[46] Ibid

expertise to India, to crush the uprising in Kashmir, point towards an Indo-Israeli nexus directed against Pakistan.[47]

Israeli US supplied Apache attack helicopter

Pakistani MBT on exercise

---

[47] Ammar, op cit:2

Had India attacked Pakistani nuclear installations in 1984, it undoubtedly would have initiated a full-scale war. Pakistan would have retaliated in kind against an Indian nuclear installation. The region was simply lucky it escaped a fourth war.[48]

Pakistan's army Nasr battlefield short range nuclear capable missile

[48] India, Israel almost attacked Kahuta: report -
https://www.pakistantoday.com.pk/2015/10/26/india-israel-almost-attacked-kahuta-report/

Image/pexels.com/F-16 Falcon silhouette

References

Arnett, Nuclear stability and arms sales to India, Arms Control Today, 1997

Ashok Kapur, Pakistan's attitude to the NPT, Parchment Press, 1993

Chapter Six: Asia, 2018, The Military Balance, vol. 118, no. 1, pp. 219

Chris Bishop, Encyclopedia of Air Warfare-Volume 2, Aerospace Publishing Ltd, 1997

Christopher Walker and Michael Evans, Pakistan Feared Israeli Raid, The Times, Wednesday June 3, 1998

Christopher Walker, Israel's Helped India for 20 years, The Times, Thursday June 4, 1998

Cordesman, A.H. (1988). Armed Forces Journal, Western Strategic Interests and the India-Pakistan military balance, Ian Allan Ltd.

David Albright and Tom Zamora, India and Pakistan go Nuclear, Bulletin of Atomic Scientists, 1989

Davis, Paul. 2009. *Giving up the bomb: motivations and incentives*. [Online]. Available at: http://carleton.ca/npsia/wpcontent/uploads/davis_bomb.pdf Dawn Weekly, Kashmir Policy, Touch Media Co.Ltd, 1998

Defence.pk - https://defence.pk/

Eric Arnett, Delhi able to play nuclear trump in game for control of Kashmir, The Times, May 1998

Eric Arnett, Military Capacity and the Risk of War-China, India, Pakistan and Iran, Oxford University Press, 1997

Eric Arnett, What Threat?, Bulletin of the Atomic Scientists, 1997

Freedman, L. (1985). Atlas of Global Strategy, MacMillan London Ltd. Freedman, Lawrence. 2003. The Evolution of Nuclear Strategy. 3rd ed. New York: Palgrave Macmillan.

Global Security - https://www.globalsecurity.org/

Government of Pakistan, Ministry of Defence - http://www.mod.gov.pk/

Hafeez Malik, Dilemmas of National Security and Co-operation, The Macmillan Press Ltd, 1993

IISS, Strategic Survey 2013 – The Annual Review of World Affairs, Routledge, 2013

Impact International, Delhi Expands its Strategic Swath, News & Media Ltd, 1996

Imtiaz Bakhari, The beginning of another 'Great Game'?, Jang Publishers Ltd, September 26, 1998

India Today, India and Pakistan hours away from a nuclear war, 1994

India Today, India is now a nuclear weapon state, Living India Media Ltd,

May 1998

India Today, Pakistan's nuclear test, what now, June 1998

Indian Air Force - http://indianairforce.nic.in/

Indian Army - https://indianarmy.nic.in/index.aspx

Indian Navy - https://www.indiannavy.nic.in/

Inter Services Public Relations (ISPR) - https://www.ispr.gov.pk/

International Institute for Strategic Studies (IISS), Military Balance 1998-99, Oxford University Press, 1998

J.A.S Greenville, History of the World, HarperCollins Publishers, 1994

J.Goldstein & J. Pevehouse, International Relations, United States, 2007
Jane Nolan, Ballistic Missiles in the Third World, Brookings Institutions, 1991

JDW, A Loss of Momentum, 1997

JDW, A Loss of Momentum, 1997

JDW, Asia's Missile Race Hots Up, 1994

JDW, Asia's Missile Race Hots Up, 1994

JDW, Country Survey- Pakistan, 1992

JDW, Country Survey-India, 1990

JDW, Country Survey-Pakistan, 1992

JDW, Fighting on the Roof of the World, 1998

JDW, IAF Follows up on Su-30 Offer, 1994

JDW, India and Pakistan move to prevent nuclear disaster, March 1999

JDW, India becomes Sixth Nuclear Weapons State, 1998

JDW, India Budget May Affect Modernisation, 1998

JDW, India's Search for a New SPG, 1994

JDW, Indian Budget Fall May Affect Modernisation, 1998

JDW, Latest Tests put India in Nuclear Arms Spotlight, 1998

JDW, Mounting Tensions in South Asia, 1996

JDW, Nuclear Submarine is being built in India, December 1994

JDW, Pakistan Needs up to 70 Nuclear Warheads, June 1998

JDW, Pakistan's Time for Reassessment, 1998

JDW, Trials Provide Data for Range of Weapons Yields, 1998

Kapur, S. Paul. 2007. Dangerous Deterrent: Nuclear Weapons Proliferation and Conflict in South Asia. Palo Alto, Calif, Stanford University Press.

Kazmi, Zahir. 2010. *Neo-nuclear apartheid.* [Online]. Available at: http://www.dawn.com/news/594849/neo-nuclear-apartheid

Lawrence Freedman, Atlas of Global Strategy, Macmillan Press Ltd, 1985

Lawrence Freedman, National Pride sets the Sabre Rattling, Daily Mail, May 29, 1998

Liberman, Peter. 2008. Israel and the South African bomb. New York. The Nonproliferation Review.

Mahnaz Ipahani, Pakistan: dimensions of insecurity, Brassey's, 1990

Maleeha Lodhi, Nuclear Risk reduction and Conflict-Resolution in South Asia, Jang Publications Ltd, 1998

Mustaq Ali Khan, Pakistan Army Green Book, Ferozsons (Pvt) Ltd, 1990

News International, Advani's Nuclear Blackmail, August 10, 1998

News International, India will have to reclaim Azaad Kashmir says Defence Minister, Jang Publications Ltd, 1998

News International, Nuclear arms not to be used: Nawaz, June 1998

Norris, Robert S. and Hans M. Kristensen. 2005. British Nuclear Forces, 2005. Bulletin of the Atomic Scientists.

Official Gateway To The Government Of Pakistan -

http://www.pakistan.gov.pk/index.html

Pakistan Air Force - http://www.paf.gov.pk/

Paul Rogers, Guide to Nuclear Weapons 1984-85, C.J.W Printers Ltd, 1984

Peter G. Tsourus, Changing Orders-The Evolution of the World's Armies, Arms and Armour Press, 1994

Pixabay https://pixabay.com/en/photos/?q=military&image_type=&cat=&min_height=&min_width=&order=popular&pagi=2

Sean Kay, Global Security in the Twenty-First Century, Rowman & Littlefield Publishers, Inc, 2006

SIPRI - https://www.sipri.org/

SIPRI Yearbook (2014) – Armaments, Disarmament and International Security, Oxford University Press Inc., New York.

Tarock, Adam, 2006, Iran's Nuclear Programme and the West, *Third World Quarterly*, Vol. 27 (4), Routledge Taylor & Francis Ltd.

Tarun Basu, Selective Satellite Tracking of Missiles Alledged, India Abroad, 1997

The Daily Telegraph, Nuclear Blasts Puts Pakistan in Arms Race, 1998

The Times, Pakistan Blasts into the Arms Race, Times Newspaper Ltd, 1998

Tsourus, Peter G. 1994. Changing Orders-The Evolution of the World's Armies. London. Armies and Armour Press.

Y. Ammar, The Kashmir Factor, Palestine Times, 9 October 1991

Zachary S. Davis. 2011. The India-Pakistan Military Standoff. New York. Palgrave Macmillan Press.

Zian Mian, No time to think, Jang Publishers Ltd, 1998

Images in this book fall under the following categories

(a) public domain (applicable to most official photos released by the military/manufacturers)

(b) free for commercial use

(c) used with explicit permission from the owner (applicable to all images from private websites)

(d) assumed to fall under (a) or (b) (applicable to images in printed media where no image owner is identified)

INDEX

A

Air Marshal M. Anwar Shamim · 36
Andrew Korybko · 11
AWACS · 43

B

BJP government · 13

C

Cyber attacks · 9

D

Dimona nuclear reactor · 39
Dr Abdul Kalam · 44

E

Economic · 9

G

General Qamar Javed Bajwa · 8

H

Hybrid war · 9

I

India · 12
Indira Gandhi · 25
Iran-Iraq war · 18
ISI · 35
Islamabad · 33
Israel · 31
Israeli F-16 · 17
Israeli Mossad · 24

J

Jamnagar · 42
Jamnagar airfield · 25
Jane's Information Group · 46
Jordanian · 17

K

Kahuta · 21
KANUPP · 40

M

Major General Ivry · 43
Menachem Begin · 15
Mirza Aslam Beg · 40

N

New Delhi · 35

O

Operation Opera · 16
Operation Orchard' · 20
Osirak · 16

P

Pakistan Air Force · 24
Pakistan Map · vii
Paul Beaver · 46
Political · 9

R

RAW · 24

S

Societal · 9

T

Tel Aviv · 35

Trombay · 24

Tuwaitha complex · 16

Recently released books (2018)

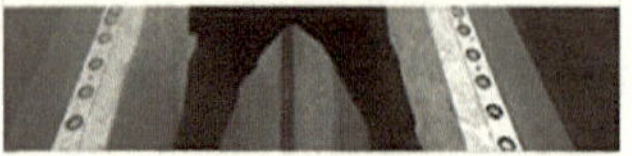

Major changes in East Asia have placed the region near the top of the World's strategic agenda. East Asia has until recently experienced the fastest regional economic growth rate in the world for many years. Economic co-operation has been flourishing and economic interests have become the major reason in reshaping East Asian international relations. However, there have also been changes in the security environment, due to many factors, such as the reduction of US forces in East Asia, the

56

disintegration of the Soviet Union (the decline of the Soviet Union's presence in the region had led to renewed attention to traditional and potential rivalries among the major East Asian powers), and the concern of China's hegemonistic ambitions.

Product details

- **Paperback:** 106 pages
- **Publisher:** CreateSpace Independent Publishing Platform; 1 edition (16 Jan. 2018)
- **Language:** English
- **ISBN-10:** 1974062309
- **ISBN-13:** 978-1974062300
- **Product Dimensions:** 21.6 x 0.6 x 27.9 cm

The astronomical rising costs of modern combat has resulted in many countries being deprived of purchasing a modern combat aircraft and this has had an adverse effect on their security. Many nations have tried to undertake cost-effective measures for their defence needs.

Countries can either purchase very expensive modern aircraft or buy older aircraft that can be expensive to operate due to their high maintenance requirements. The Pakistan Air Force had initiated the plan to co-develop an affordable modern multi-role fighter aircraft with China. Chengdu Aircraft Corporation (CAC) in collaboration with Pakistan Aeronautical Complex (PAC, Kamra) have jointly developed the JF-17 Thunder combat aircraft (also known as the FC-1 Xiaolong Fierce Dragon in China).

JF-17 Thunder is a sophisticated light-weight multi-role, all weather, day/night fighter aircraft that is manufactured by Pakistan and China. The JF-17 Thunder has become a very cost-effective aircraft that costs very little compared to other modern aircraft. Many countries have shown an interest and a few have started to make orders. Some have described the JF-17 as the 'Ultimate MiG-21' arguing that the Chinese/Pakistani JF-17 builds on a classic warplane – although it has no resemblance and its level of sophistication is comparable to current advanced fighter aircraft on the market. This very modern and capable aircraft has the potential to become a potent platform that can serve with numerous air forces across the world. Product details

- **Paperback:** 178 pages
- **Publisher:** CreateSpace Independent Publishing Platform (26 Feb. 2018)
- **Language:** English
- **ISBN-10:** 1984055240
- **ISBN-13:** 978-1984055248
- **Product Dimensions:** 21.6 x 1.1 x 27.9 cm

The global security challenges after the post-Cold war period has affected many countries. Pakistan's geography and location present its security planners with serious, almost irresolvable strategic and tactical problems. It borders the nuclear states of India and China, an ambitious Iran, and an unstable Afghanistan, which is perceived as a gateway to its commercial-strategic ambitions in Central Asia.

Pakistan's key security problems are a reflection of its history and domestic circumstances. The overriding concern of Pakistan is its internal and external security. Strategically, Pakistan lacks territorial depth. Its main cities and communication routes are relatively close to the border with India and are susceptible to attack. In addition, the headwaters of Pakistan's rivers and main irrigation systems originate from India. Pakistan's borders with India were also new and mainly unfortified and, in many places, were drawn in ways that made them indefensible. Because the borders were also un-demarcated, there was abundant chance for conflict. Pakistan has particularly been affected with a number of issues.

It has been argued by many that a Fourth generation/Hybrid war has been imposed on Pakistan, in order to break the nation (Balkanization of Pakistan into different parts) with the aim of making it either extremely weak or total destruction as a nation state (so that it is not able to challenge the hegemonistic ambitions of its adversaries).The purpose of this book is to assess the military security problems that Pakistan faces, and focus on its external security matters (military threats from neighbouring countries such as India, balance of power in the region, nuclear and ballistic missile threats, relationship with external powers, the high risk of war and its role on the 'War on Terror'), and its internal security problems (sectarianism, proliferation of small arms, refugees, ethnic violence, drug problem, economic weaknesses), and also its ability to cope with these problems.

Product details

- **Paperback:** 366 pages
- **Publisher:** CreateSpace Independent Publishing Platform; 1 edition (13 April 2018)
- **Language:** English
- **ISBN-10:** 1986169421
- **ISBN-13:** 978-1986169424
- **Product Dimensions:** 21.6 x 2.2 x 27.9 cm

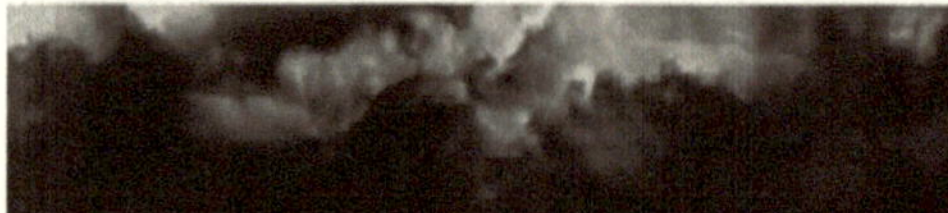

An impending nuclear holocaust is likely to happen, if the world community does not take action. A conflict that has been simmering for many years is beginning to spiral out of control. Two nuclear powers have an unresolved dispute that has increased tensions in the region.

Both countries are purchasing and developing sophisticated state-of-the-art weapons that could unleash great terror and destruction on the populations of both countries – with also serious global ramifications.

The world's most dangerous flashpoint, has the highest chance of a nuclear war occurring – it is deemed by many to be more serious that the Cuban Missile Crisis and North Korea's nuclear sabre rattling. The dispute needs to be amicably resolved between both nations and confidence building measures need to be implemented.

Product details

- **Paperback:** 154 pages
- **Publisher:** CreateSpace Independent Publishing Platform; 1 edition (16 April 2018)
- **Language:** English
- **ISBN-10:** 1717040403
- **ISBN-13:** 978-1717040404
- **Product Dimensions:** 21.6 x 0.9 x 27.9 cm

KAHUTA: THE INDO-ISRAELI PLAN TO ATTACK PAKISTAN'S NUCLEAR PLANT

Pakistan faces a number of threats from internal and external forces – with the aim of weakening the country and an attempt to 'balkanise' Pakistan in to different parts. The Pakistani Chief of Army, General Qamar Javed Bajwa has said that "a hybrid war had been imposed on Pakistan to internally weaken it, but noted that the enemies were failing to divide the country on the basis of ethnicity and other identities".

Furthermore he states, "Our enemies know that they cannot beat us fair and square and have thus subjected us to a cruel, evil and protracted hybrid war. They are trying to weaken our resolve by weakening us from within". Conflicts in Ukraine, Israel and Lebanon (Hizbullah), Syria, Libya, War on Terror in Afghanistan and its impact in Pakistan etc., have resulted in multi-layered efforts to destabilise a functioning state and polarize its society. The centre of gravity is to target population in hybrid warfare. The aim of the adversary is to influence influential policy makers and key decision makers by combining kinetic operations with subversive efforts. The aggressor often resorts to covert actions, to avoid attribution or retribution. At the moment there is no universally accepted definition of hybrid wars – the term is too abstract and is seen by some as using a fancy term to refer to irregular methods to counter conventionally stronger forces.

Accordingly, many say that the new definitions of 4th generation or hybrid wars are really the repackaging of the traditional clash between the armed forces of nation states and the non-state insurgents. This book will be assessing Pakistan's insecurity and the hybrid wars imposed onto it by its adversaries. It will look at a number of issues that Pakistan is facing (military imbalance, economic and political weaknesses, internal and external security threats and the impact of hybrid warfare on Pakistan).

Product details

- **Paperback:** 132 pages
- **Publisher:** CreateSpace Independent Publishing Platform; 1 edition (17 Jun. 2018)
- **Language:** English
- **ISBN-10:** 1721510095
- **ISBN-13:** 978-1721510092
- **Product Dimensions:** 21.6 x 0.8 x 27.9 cm

Each year billions of dollars' worth of arms are procured between various nations, despite the fact that many millions of people live in desperate poverty, many will die from hunger and hunger related diseases. Weapons of increasing firepower and the missiles to deliver them accurately are being acquired, mainly through the Global Arms Trade. This means that we must expect wars in the world to become increasingly violent and destructive.

This book focuses on what the arms trade is and its impact on the world, the wars which have resulted or were sustained by this trade. It is necessary to know which countries sell arms and which ones buy. Also it is important to have some idea of how large the trade is. The international trade in arms has considerably increased since World War 2. Major weapons (aircraft, missiles, tanks and ships) probably account for about one-half of the total trade in weapons and equipment. Many countries and their respective Military-Industrial Complex are 'making a killing' in the world's largest trade in the buying and selling of military technology (weapons).

Product details

- **Paperback:** 90 pages
- **Publisher:** CreateSpace Independent Publishing Platform (28 July 2018)
- **Language:** English
- **ISBN-10:** 1721773150
- **ISBN-13:** 978-1721773152
- **Product Dimensions:** 15.2 x 0.5 x 22.9 cm

The global security challenges since World War II and thereafter (post-Cold war period) has affected many countries. This has resulted in a number of countries pursuing a nuclear weapons programme to provide them with the ultimate security – the belief that the fear of utter annihilation of their opponents would result in deterrence and eventually detente. According to Kristensen and Norris (2014), there are approximately 16,300 nuclear weapons located at some 97 sites in 14 countries. Many of these weapons are in military arsenals (roughly 10,000), with the remaining ones being in the process of retirement and awaiting dismantlement. Accordingly, 93% of the total global inventory resides in Russia and the United States of America. The remaining weapon stockpiles are in the United Kingdom (UK), France, China, India, Pakistan, North Korea and Israel.

This book looks at the proliferation of weapons of mass destruction (WMD), the double standards and hypocrisy practiced by the five declared nuclear powers. It gives a brief short history of nuclear development in the nuclear countries and the impact of nuclear war. It argues that the only way to eradicate these horrendous weapons is for the five declared nuclear powers to make immediate measures to dismantle the weapons and stockpiles of weaponised materials – as they had agreed under the Nuclear Non-proliferation Treaty (NPT).

Product details

- **Paperback:** 146 pages
- **Publisher:** CreateSpace Independent Publishing Platform (31 July 2018)
- **Language:** English
- **ISBN-10:** 1983910414
- **ISBN-13:** 978-1983910418
- **Product Dimensions:** 15.2 x 0.8 x 22.9 cm

This book looks at the concept of 'terrorism' and its primary aim of creating a climate of fear. Any discussion of terrorism has to firstly define its terms: what do we mean by terrorism and how does it manifest itself in contemporary accounts and moreover, what is the difference between legitimate military action and one based on terror? The definitions of terrorism are complex and depend, to a very large extent, on who one is asking. A government defence adviser would, for instance, have a markedly different notion of what constitutes terrorism than a member of a paramilitary organisation and an ordinary member of the public might have a notion based somewhere on the interaction between these two depending on their socio-cultural background. This is primarily the main reason why the term has not been universally accepted by all scholars or academics.

There are many reasons why political groups attempt to bring about radical change through terrorism. People are often frustrated with their position in society. They may in some way feel persecuted or oppressed because of their race, religion, or they feel exploited by a government. Any group that uses terrorist actions have very complex and powerful reasons to engage in those activities. The usual experience of violence by a stronger party has historically turned victims into terrorists. State terror very often breeds collective terror. Because 'terrorism' is a word that has been used so much and so loosely that it has lost a clear meaning. It can be argued that terrorists are not born, but created as issues of today develop into the conflicts of tomorrow.

Product details

- **Paperback:** 202 pages
- **Publisher:** CreateSpace Independent Publishing Platform (7 Aug. 2018)
- **Language:** English
- **ISBN-10:** 1724714856
- **ISBN-13:** 978-1724714855
- **Product Dimensions:** 15.2 x 1.2 x 22.9 cm

When NATO was founded in 1949, it had a clearly defined role. The demise of the Cold War, the disintegration of the Soviet Union and the collapse of communism in the period from 1989 to 1991 called into question NATO's future role and its continued existence. The primary role was called into question over its future relevance in the post-Cold War world. The reason for NATO was essentially a military alliance to deter Soviet and Warsaw Pact aggression – however, once the threat had finished its role had been challenged by many academics and governments. Many analysts felt that NATO was nothing more than an out of date alliance from the Cold War with no real future. Others would say, however, that an organisation such as NATO was still crucial in the modern world to ensure that countries do not act unilaterally, but co-operate with allies. In view of the situations, NATO has managed to address new issues and adapt its roles on different levels.

- **Paperback:** 66 pages
- **Publisher:** CreateSpace Independent Publishing Platform (10 Aug. 2018)
- **Language:** English
- **ISBN-10:** 1725092816
- **ISBN-13:** 978-1725092815
- **Product Dimensions:** 15.2 x 0.4 x 22.9 cm

Tony Wilkinson was a small time crook and a thief - and not very successful at that. He was called 'fate' by anybody who knew him due to these reasons. Because, it seemed, fate had dealt a nasty blow to his occupation, and to him. Because every job he ever pulled, backfired on him and had proved to be costly for him. Things were going to change after he made a plan to improve his situation. However, his plan came up with unexpected hurdles. He then looked at his past and fate asked the question to himself, "What chance did I stand against Kismet?"

- **Paperback:** 33 pages
- **Publisher:** Independently published (8 Dec. 2018)
- **Language:** English
- **ISBN-10:** 1790958296
- **ISBN-13:** 978-1790958290
- **Product Dimensions:** 15.2 x 0.2 x 22.9 cm

KAHUTA: THE INDO-ISRAELI PLAN TO ATTACK PAKISTAN'S NUCLEAR
PLANT

ABOUT THE AUTHOR

Saghir Iqbal is a researcher in International Relations and Security Studies. He is an experienced Intelligence Analyst and has achieved a number of qualifications in this field. He is also a Lecturer in Business Management as well as an Examiner for A Level History and Business. Saghir Iqbal has a subject specialism in the following areas:

International Politics of the Cold War 1945-1991
Conflict Resolution in International Society+
Global and North-South Security Studies
Britain in the World
Disarmament Processes: History and Theory
Nationalism and Ethnicity in Post-Cold War Politics
Middle East: Area in Conflict
European Security
International Politics of the Environment
The United Nations, Peacekeeping and Intervention
Disarmament Processes: Current Problems
Globalisation and the South
International Terrorism
International Politics and Security Studies
Introduction to Peace Studies
Politics of the Global Environment
Regional Security in East Asia
Critical Security studies

Recently released books (2018)

- Dangerous Flashpoints in East Asia: The Military Build-up
- JF-17 Thunder: The Making of a Modern Cost- effective Multi-role Combat Aircraft
- Pakistan's War Machine: An Encyclopedia of its Weapons, Strategy and Military Security
- Miscalculation: Risks of Inadvertent Nuclear War
- Hybrid Warfare and its Impact on Pakistan's Security
- Making a Killing: The Scourge of the Global Arms Trade
- Nuclear Apartheid: Bullying, Hypocrisy and the Double Standards on Nuclear Weapons
- Terrorism: Creating a Climate of Fear

Website: www.saghir.co.uk